Crossroads

10 OCT 09

Crossroads

To Lisa + Shawn,

May you inspire each other throughout your lives together and may God bless you richley. May you also find inspiration within the pages of this book. The best to you both as you travel on your new journey together.

Only from the heart
Your cousin
Allan Finnegan

Allan Finnegan

Copyright © 2008 by Allan Finnegan.

Library of Congress Control Number: 2007908645
ISBN: Hardcover   978-1-4363-0069-8
               Softcover   978-1-4363-0068-1

All rights reserved. No part of this book may be reproduced or transmitted in any form or by any means, electronic or mechanical, including photocopying, recording, or by any information storage and retrieval system, without permission in writing from the copyright owner.

This book was printed in the United States of America.

To order additional copies of this book, contact:
Xlibris Corporation
1-888-795-4274
www.Xlibris.com
Orders@Xlibris.com

Contents

Acknowledgements 11

This Mountain 13
Sunshine 14
Indians Lament 15
The Boys in the Band 17
Manifest Destiny 19
A Passions Pain 21
Realms of Reason/Child's Innocence 22
Mountain Top Castles 23
The Homecoming 24
Distant Shores 26
The Dawn of Night 27
Footprints 28
Passion 29
Take Me to the Country 30
The Window 31
Outlook 32
Moving On 33
Fade to Night 35
In Quiet Moments 36
Alone at Last 37
Scenes of Life 38
Without Any Lies 39
Dragon's Breath 41
I Want You 42
If I Should Leave 43
Whispers of a Foreign Wind 44
Come and Go 45
Passages of Time 46
Alaska 48

Oh Father	49
Starting to Fall	50
Saying Good-Bye	51
Trying to tell You	53
The Beauty of You	54
Chords of Life	55
A Change is Near	56
Too Little, Too Late	57
Tribulations	58
Buckroe Beach, Va.	59
Retrospect	60
The Silent Rapture	61
Burning Passion Flight	62
The City Sleeps	63
The Silent Scream	64
Blue Moon	65
Interlude	66
Climbing High	67
Nocturnal Pleasure	68
Childhood Lost	69
First Embrace	70
This Passage	71
Don't Look Now	72
One Dream	74
If You Have To Leave	76
Once and Then	77
Look at the Night	78
Different Drummer	79
Your Eyes	80
Take Me Away	81
But For a Kiss	82
Lonely State of Mind	83
In the Land of Dreams	85
A Love Gone By	87
Crossroads	89
A Bright Tomorrow	90
Forever and a Day	91
If I Could Change the World	92
Grand Canyon	93

Crazy	94
If I Could Find the Words to Tell You	95
Some People	96
Moody Girl	98
If Dreams Had Wings	100
Stand By You	102
Find My Way	104
Motorcycle Mama	105
Winners and Losers	106
New Birth	107

Dedication

To Jeannette, Paula, and Donna.

Acknowledgements

First, I would like to thank the Creator for giving me this wonderful and special gift that I now share with you. It is by His grace I am able to write such words allowing me to touch others in a way that comes only from the heart. I would like to thank my immediate family for their love, support, and encouragement. To my mother Jeannette, my sisters, Paula and Donna you are the best and my love for you only grows with each day. I want to thank my mother, Jeannette, for giving me the greatest gift. I would like to let my sisters know that I am very proud of their own accomplishments. To my son Joshua whose knowledge of music is extraordinary, I am so proud. Follow your dream.

To my nieces and nephews, Johnny, Summer, Autumn, Holly, Andrew, Heather, Hannah, and Katherine who have been nothing but pure joy in my life. To my father Gilbert Socia and his wife Thelma, your humor, wit, and stories will always remain an integral part of me. You have been a great part of my life.

I would like to give thanks to all my friends and extended family on the Powwow trail that over the years have been there and have listened to the pains of a growing poet and friend both in small and big ways. You have all been a blessing in my life. To Chuck and Zandra Cline and Frank and Kim Altomare I cherish the memory of when we first met and how I have come to know you through the years. To Stephen Standing Owl whose beautiful flute music is an inspiration in and of it-self. To Chuck Hagen and Bert Gunn whose wisdom and intellect have taught me much.

To Ernie Proper and the Black Thunder Singers, Paul Burke and the Four Winds Singers, Al Caron and the Walking Bear Singers, and the Bullock Family, Paul, Marion, Andy, Chris, and Ed where would the Powwow season be without you? To my dear and wonderful friends Dave and Rose Holloman who have been there through these years all the way from Virginia Beach. To Sue McKeon who has been a very best friend for many years whose opinion

I hold and admire much. It would not be the same without you. To Christina Jackmauh who has been my best critic and dear friend whose knowledge of the arts surpasses many. To Cecile Potvin and Angela DeFreitas whose friendship and kindness have been a cherished pleasure.

If I have left anyone out by name it is an over sight on my part as there are many too numerous to mention. All of you have touched my life as I can only hope I have touched yours. I love you all. Thank you for being who you are and being a part of my life.

Allan Finnegan

This Mountain

I thought I would climb
That mountain one day
The one I've seen so often
The one that touched the sky

I stood at the foot
Looked up and wondered
How long will it take
A day, a month, eternity
I'm climbing now
The days linger on
Is the top just beyond

This mountain
What purpose it serves
To look at, amaze, behold
To climb higher, to reach it's peak
To suffer in defeat
This mountain beckons
Come take me on
A challenge that has no wrong

It has me now
No turning back
Onward I do climb
This mountain
The one I've seen so often
The one that touched the sky

Sunshine

The birds flew
The wind blew
And the air breathed

The sun shone
From its throne
Down upon the living

There it glistened
Giving life anew

Indians Lament

Eagles soaring
Rivers flowing
Thunder roaring
Mountains held on high

    Horses running chasing the wind
    Buffalo herds are back again
    Drum beats for dancing
    Warriors prancing
    The wail of the war cry

        Valleys wide
        Plains vast
        Dreams of the vision quest are cast
        Now is the time of the sun dance
        The mark of endurance to always last

            Counting coup
            Buffalo stew
            The thrill of the hunt
            Drying meat on the racks
            Pretty woman with papoose on their backs

                Medicine man's magic
                Casting his spell
                Making the sick become well
                Children playing in the fields
                Bows and arrows and painted war shields

They loved their freedom
They loved their land
This they would give to no man
They fought and died for what they believed in
And the white man called it sin

    Broken promises, traveled miles, a trail of tears
    Sand Creek, the Washita, Wounded Knee
    Desert reservations, longing to be free

        Indian chiefs lead their people
        Sitting Bull, Red Cloud, Dull Knife
        Chief Joseph, Cochise, and Black Kettle
        Gall, Crazy Horse, and Geronimo too
        All do the Ghost dance
        The dream of one last chance

            This land is theirs now
            As long as the rivers run
            And the grass shall grow

The Boys in the Band

Here they come now the boys in the band
Let's all stand and give them a hand

    Crosby and Stills had Nash and Young
    Here we go now the fun has just begun
    ZZ Top sings with a Texas drawl
    The Beach Boys played Chicago and had a ball

Elton John came down the Yellow Brick Road
All his roadies had a heavy load
Yes staged a concert with ELP
The Moody Blues had to come out to see

    Meatloaf sang like a Bat out of Hell
    Billy Idol shouted the Rebel Yell
    There was a Storm at Sunup for Vanelli fans
    Billy Joel the Big Shot was caught in the stands

Queen will rock you and Tie Your Mother Down
The Stones will start you up when they come to town
Steely Dan played those Deacon Blues
Supertramps' Breakfast in America was all over the news

    You got Charlie Daniels playing his fiddle
    Well the cow jumped over the moon hey diddle diddle
    You got Klemmer and Barbieri playing their jazz
    Here's the Little River Band Reminiscing to add the pizzazz

Now Aerosmith with Dream On enters your dreams
All these rock stars playing in streams
Can't You See Marshall Tucker come riding in
Giddy up them horses and pass the gin

    Van Halen and Nugent hear them sing
    Playing their guitars burning up the string
    Genesis came over from across the sea
    They sang Suppers Ready lets all have some tea

Styx rode down the river singing their songs
They said Come Sail Away it won't be for long
Boz Scaggs did the Lido Shuffle playing his piano
Mandy, This One's for You said Manilow

Now one more word before it's time to go
Cause they are still putting on a great big show
Thanks to Otis, Marvin, and Sam Cook too, they gave us so much
We will forever feel their loving touch

    Don't forget Holley or Hendrix they had their say
    For Croce and Morrison it was their life's way
    Elvis and Darrin sang along with the rest
    They were right up there playing with the best

For the rest of the boys they are not forgotten
They are playing too
They are still up there making their stand and
We all know Grand Funk is just an American Band

Manifest Destiny

North wind blowing across the plains
Buffalo herds, tumbleweed, broken weather vanes
Wagon wheels rolling forever-moving west
Beaten trails to follow slowly at their best

    The Santa Fe and Oregon Trail
    Pony express riders carry the mail
    Outlaws in the badlands robbing banks
    Marshals bringing them in receiving thanks

Land so beautiful the eyes behold
The forty-niners striking gold
Iron horse is moving across the land
To white eyes the Indian is a mystery man

    Indian villages the eyes can see
    Custer and the Little Big Horn, don't tread on me
    Red Cloud stood tall among the Sioux
    The Black Hills were theirs under the great wide blue

Chivington met Black Kettle at the Sand Creek
There was no mercy for the strong or the weak
Two hundred people massacred that day
Most, woman and children, none buried where they lay

    The Wagon Box Fight and the Fetterman massacre
    Sign of the times they are getting what they are after
    Tecumseh Sherman stood his ground
    Surrender, or be nowhere to be found

Fighting Apaches had Crook on the run
His men called them devils but they sure had their fun
Crazy Horse and Sitting Bull murdered in cold blood
Geronimo surrendered and the white man came in floods

    Manifest destiny had its say
    The white man came in a genocidal way
    The Indian people fought for their right
    The white man showed who had the might

Now those great warriors of old
Whose stories still are told
Will always live in the hearts of the young
They have risen up to meet the sun

"They made us many promises, more than I can remember,
They kept but one, they promised to take our land
And they took it"
              -Redcloud

A Passions Pain

Pent up emotions
That long to live
Are caught inside
Wanting to give

Loneliness clings to the soul
Like grapes on a vine
People search for love
That they cannot find

Lonely hearts cry for love
But have none
Restless hunger
Inflames everyone

Meaningless relationships
Are all so vain
While lonely hearts suffer
In a passions pain

Realms of Reason/Child's Innocence

Realms of reason
Search the vacant mind
To brave new offerings
Is not to be confined
Experience breeds
One's life anew
To search the depths
Is up to you

Flowers blossom
In the day light sun
New life has begun
As man's maturity
Shows his face
A new child's
Innocence
Whispers grace

Mountain Top Castles

Sweet jasmine fragrance
Breathes the air as
Mountain valley springs
Awaken to dawn's morning mist
Listless winds drape the
Forest's majesty
Where eagles fly
Soaring among the clouds
Distant echoes of
Slumbering thunder
Deepens my soul
While shadows run free
To play with the sun
In calm serenity
There on mountain top castles
I become a babe
In mother nature's arms
Succulent to her life
That surrounds me

The Homecoming

I heard that train come calling
She was running down the track
The lonesome whistle blew
As thoughts cascaded back

So many years and so many miles
Of travels far and wide
New horizons led me
I sailed the surging tide

From mountain peaks and valleys
To pastures green and desert sands
I traveled seas and saw the wonder
Of a thousand foreign lands

Now my journey has brought me back
To the place where I belong
I guess I always knew it
It never was this strong

I longed for you a thousand times
A burning passion, one of a kind
I remembered how you felt to me
So wrapped up in thoughts of mind

I've changed I know, you have too
We grew up worlds apart
Life's freedom showed the way
For others though it is just a start

I thank your heart for waiting
Though I don't know why
Perhaps it was you knew
The voyager must die

As I board this train one last time
That lonesome whistle blows
I turn my head for one last look
To the road that always knows

I'm coming home now can't you see
I've found that place where I long to be

Distant Shores

The child dreamed of wisdom
He hoped to gain someday
But didn't want to venture
For the price he had to pay

Lonely hearts dreamt
For love not to die
Dreams on forgotten faces
Showed with hope
In a babies first cry

The rich man dreamt of freedom
Trapped in the monetary darkness
From the things he could not see
The poor man dreamt of wealth
And what he wanted to be
Trapped in the consciousness
Of his insecurity

As the old man dreamt of youth
Lost in a moments time
He saw those things that were
And what he couldn't find

Then I sailed the rivers
To the seas of things to be
I saw on faces passing
The harrowed look
Of perplexity

And the light shone
To those distant shores

The Dawn of Night

Autumn's cool breeze
Flutters through
Towering pines

As the evening sun's rays
Sparkle mountain streams
One last caress

The ebb of dusk quiets
Forest life to
New serenity

And in the
Dawn of night
Stars shine one by one
To paint pictures
In the sky

Footprints

Moonbeams shine
To summer
Midnight dreams
Fantasies of worlds
Once lived long ago

The ocean's silence roars
Caressing deserted
Sandy beaches
Where mornings mist
Fades against
The rising sun

Revealing footprints
In the sand
And the memory
Of you

Passion

Passion is a madness
Feeling so alive
Like melodious rhythm
Gloriously it thrives
Happy is this feeling
Madness all untold
To the hearts content
Joyous to behold

Passion is a madness
Feeling life so real
Compared to natures beauty
Pleasantly to feel
Full of so much ecstasy
No illusionary mind
Feeling life of love is
Like no other kind

Take Me to the Country

Take me to the mountaintops
Or the open sea
Take me to deep valleys
Where the life is free

Take me where wild rivers run
And where the eagles fly
Take me where the wolves howl
To the midnight sky

Take me where the long wind blows
Across the desert sand
Take me where the pine trees scent
Spills across the land

Take me to that land of honey
And sweet nature springs
Take me to that land of sunshine
Where morning warblers sing

Take me to those open spaces
Where the buffalo roam
Take me to the country
The place that I call home

The Window

Alone by the window
She sits and stares
Watching the rain in
Her rocking chair

    Chained to her demise
    With nowhere to go
    She sits and wonders
    Will anyone show

        Memories flare of
        Life once free
        How blossomed youth
        Held such tranquility

            Weathered with age
            Tears swell the eye
            No one hears her
            Lonely hearts cry

                Through the rain
                The darkness falls
                While silence echoes
                Through empty halls

                      Sitting by the window

Outlook

In the wake of time
I was a child
Innocence bled
Of life anew

As seasons passed
I became a man
On the eve of new
Tomorrows

And when night
Turned to day
Never again did I
See things as
I saw them

Yesterday
Or the day before

Moving On

Whispering wind
Shuffles through the trees
Unknown stillness lies
Clouds break as midnights chariot
Points the way to freedoms open road

Time to keep on moving
The feeling is in the air
Don't like confines of city life
The walls can tear you down
Don't like crowded busy streets
Another losing race track meet

Give me those wide-open spaces
The home of scenic no time places
I'm going to take the high road
I have to keep moving on
Can't you hear her voice calling
Singing that mystery song

The wind is blowing stronger now
Mountains live forever
Honeysuckle fills the air
The valley is carpet green
I'm going to ride that golden rail
To some new sunset never seen

I'm going to find new meaning
Of what life holds for me
Another new experience
I'll sail the open sea
If we should meet in passing
We can reminisce on
Our journeys shared

A rosy red sun
On a blue horizon
Sparks the twilight sky
Give me those wide-open spaces
The home of scenic no time places
I have to keep moving on

Fade To Night

Fade to night
Delirium's face of
Fortitude
Silence walks a
Lonely path of
Passion and despair
Caught in the web of
Haughty nothingness
The seeds of time are rare

Stillborn
So incessant
Nighttime bleak
A forsaken lass
Quivering weeping child
Hard like swords of steel
Cutting deep, surreal

Fade to night
Burning light
River of life
Darkness
Never cares

In Quiet Moments

Quiet stillness lies as
Sunshine slowly sinks
Against a purple sky
A mountain breeze blows softly
As my memory lingers there
In days of youth gone by

Thoughts of youth so lasting
Once a life so free
Like shadows of reflections
We knew no destiny
We thought we would live forever
We were all we wanted to be

We grew so subtle in our innocent ways
Time was endless in those younger days
As seasons change with the weather
Nothing lasts forever

We lost our innocence to fate's open door
The youth that held us became no more
The world took us in her arms
To what we've come to be
No longer just reflections
We became all of what we see

The mountain stream is silent
The moon is growing bright
To me it's not a mystery
But another light
In these quiet moments
Life is not so strange
It is just the time of life
When youth has come of age

Alone At Last

Time is still
The passion burns
Another wheel slowly turns
There is no one now to follow
Now no turning back
Hope hides in the shadows
While the night waits to attack

Oh, but the vengeance
There is bittersweet
As you, loose your tongue
In the prickly heat
To those you wrong accuse
What is there to lose when
There is nothing yet to gain
To you dear friend it's all the same
One of life's last refrains
Ticks away inside

And the conscious haunts
You despise
Everything that is otherwise
Such a battle that you see
Without time to be set free
Of feelings trapped inside
You are the one set out to lose
By those you wrong accuse
Seen as you are
Fading through your wall
Of deception
Then where will you hide

The night quickens dawn on the edge of light
Silence runs adrift on a burning sea
Reflecting images of what has come to be
Out of the mist rises all things past and
You have found yourself alone at last
Alone at last

Scenes of Life

And what is life

It is the break of dawn
With morning light
A red sun setting
Against a purple sky
The rush of wind
Through towering pines
The roar of a river wild
Racing down a desert canyon

It is dew drops on
Sweetened grass
Virgin snow on a
Mountains glistening peak
A waterfalls cascade
Rising in a rainbow mist
To plush green
Valleys below

It is the stillness
Of a lake broken by
The slap of a beaver's tail
The blooming of
Flowers in spring
The softness of
Summer rain

It is a lone wolf's mourn
To a pale moon
In the silence of the night
And the seasons of
Nature's beauty
With the sound of laughter
As children play

Without Any Lies

I've been sitting here for hours trying
To write the words down that my heart wants to say
Time is still running but the clocks have all stopped
I'm in the hollows of darkness with the shadow of hope
Trying to find some new light of day

I see you on the outside and you're just looking in
Like a long forgotten dream that didn't know when to begin
Like a shadow in the distance of midsummer light
Like fog on the horizon at the edge of the night
I want to tell you that I love you but I'm all choked up
All the words have been lost in the wind
The words are haunting where do I start to begin

Maybe if you saw me, and you looked in my eyes
You would see the words written without any lies
Maybe if you saw me and you looked in my eyes
You would see the words written without any lies

Now the silence is deadly and it cuts like a knife
The words all unspoken like fire and ice
The darkness is heavy, it's taking its toll
It's icy cold walls to a bottomless hole
And hope is still glimmering in search of the light
I'm still trying to find a new sense of sight

Maybe if you saw me, and you looked in my eyes
You would see the words written without any lies
Maybe if you saw me and you looked in my eyes
You would see the words written without any lies

Then all of the answers would fall into place
The darkness would end without leaving a trace
The light would appear like a new blazing sun
All the words would be spoken without speaking one

But time is just somewhere that seems out of reach
Like being alone in a crowd at the beach
And my heart is whispering what it wants to say
As I search the darkness for some new light of day

Only if you saw me, and you looked in my eyes
You would see the words written without any lies
Only if you saw me, and you looked in my eyes
You would see the words written without any lies
You would see the words written without any lies

Dragon's Breath

The sea torments a rigid tale
Of pain and dereliction
To boundless waves
Of hovering light
Are the sights of redirection

Oh, journey through
The wake of time
Along the very finest line
Of virtue and of death
And come to know
What foretells of
The dragon's breath

Loneliness abandoned
Love that comes to all
Forsaken by the parity
When hate has come to call

Oh dragon's breath
Oh dragon's breath
Your voice of call to arms
Dispense your own viscosity
Deceptive pleasing charms

Oh, fire lighted visions
That burn throughout the night
To the eyes of mystery
Wisdom told
A ten thousand candle light

Now the sea is calm as silence
But the ripples still prevail
The ripples still prevail
The ripples still prevail

I Want You

I want you when the shades of eve are falling
When purpling shadows drift across the land
When the ocean's breeze to loving mates is calling
I want the soothing softness of your hand

I want you when the stars shine above me
And the heavens are flooded with bright moonlight
I want you with your heart and soul to love me
Throughout the wonder watches of the night

I want you when in dreams I dream
The lingering of your kiss for that old time sake
With all your gentle ways, so sweetly tender
I want you in the morning when I wake

I want you when the day is at its noontime
Sun steeped and quiet or drenched in sheets of rain
I want you when the roses bloom in June time
I want you when Autumn comes again

I want you when my soul fills with passion
I want you when I am weary or depressed
I want you when in lazy slumberous fashion
My senses need the haven of your breast

I want you through every field and wood I am roaming
I want you when I am standing on the shore
I want you when the summer birds are homing
And when they have flown, I want you more and more

I want you dear, through every changing season
I want you with a tear or with a smile
I want you more than any rhyme or reason
I want you, want you, want you
Want you, all the while

If I Should Leave

If I should leave tomorrow
Would you miss me when I'm gone
Would you think about our lives together
And how we sang life's song

Would you feel the need to tell me
That you don't want to see me go
Would you let me slip away
Instead of watching our friendship grow

Would you see the sorrow in my eyes
And feel the heart felt pain
And wonder why all the while
Of the things that can't remain

Would you see me in the distance
As a fading light
One that never faltered
That held you through the night

Would you see me as the wind
Changing with the seasons
As you search the questions for the answers
To all the unsaid reasons

Would you say those things you wanted
But never had the strength to say
Would you let the words slip by
To another forgotten day

Would you simply say good-bye
Those words that mean forever
And know inside with all your heart
That we faded away together

If I should leave tomorrow
Would you miss me when I'm gone
Would you think about our lives together
And how, we sang life's song

Whispers of a Foreign Wind

You cry for love an empty calling
Listening to whispers of a foreign wind
Life so empty all so strange but
No one hears your mourning

From the light that shines
To the shades of doubt
Simple common notions
Time has left without

Worn out desire lost in the fire
Changing seasons
Bitter to sweet, hot to cold
Chariots aflame of love grown old

The stillness and the quiet
From all to none
The tears we cry and joy we share
Meaning the same for everyone

From mirrored rippled shallow pools
To storm swept barren oceans
Cluttered tenant and barroom kept
The strands of strained emotions

Listening to whispers of a foreign wind
You hear a strange voice calling
One so deep and lost from sight
No one hears your mourning

Come and Go

We come and go like strangers
Passing in the night
We only see the surface
While searching for the light

We come and go like victims
Lost inside in the storm
Betrayed by the self indulgence
Of seeking right from wrong

We come and go so subtle
Transverse on an unfixed plain
Slipping in and out of shadows
Like some childhood game

But what is lost to reason
When doubt turns into fear
When we can't see in the justice
Why time has left us here

Do we come and go impassive
To one another's needs
Do we attempt to try harder
At one of life's less, guilty pleads

Yet we come and go in silence
With a deaf tone ear
Pretending all the while
That we really hear

As we come and go in disillusion
To what fate has held for us in store
Not really any wiser nor
The better any more

And yes, we come and go in hate
Knowing all the better
When love can choose to make it right
It must be done together

Passages of Time

They say love has a way of crumbling
Through the passages of time
Like the ocean wears away
A broken shoreline

Though we try to bridge the distance
The will just isn't there
How can we find a place that is left
That says our hearts still care

Why do memories linger
Like an open wound
When we take some things for granted
A little much too soon

Do we really wish the opposite
When the contrary is true
Only to hide our faults
Much less, accept it too

Well I say that I don't blame you
For seeking what you need
But could it be you are selfish
Out of common greed

Or maybe I am the one
Not too sensitive to care
Maybe my selfishness lacks the vision
To see the light that is there

Through these passages I have stumbled
As you are left astray
There really is no difference
Still, it is hard to make love stay

If there is no doubt without a single reason
Of decisions that were made
Why is it we regret and
Feel like it was twice paid

Now you say to me don't worry
That you understand
That we both are as guilty
To play a loaded hand

Then tell me why I feel rejected
A sense of loss and pain
Maybe I am feeling sorry
Maybe it is shame

Alaska

Dreamt about you late last night
How you left me in a shroud of mystery
Something now just isn't right
Though we are just a bit of history

Have you turned the page to close
The book on an ending chapter
And leave within not a trace
Of a memory after

Or have you since took a peek
Of how we were together
And felt again the trace of love
We could have had forever

You went off to Alaska
Chasing someone else
To distant parts unknown
I was left so broken hearted
Out here on my own

Funny how time heals all wounds
Yet the memory stays awhile
A feeling just came over me
How you touched me with your softness
And caressed me with your smile

I can't say that I miss you
Or think of you a lot
Though the years have
Passed us in between
I can't say I have forgot

Now just in case you wonder
Life has treated me fair
This painted road I travel
Still has much to bear

I guess I will stop and leave here
I hope you are doing fine
And every now and then
I come to cross your mind

Dreamt about you late last night
You went off to Alaska, Alaska, Alaska

Oh Father

Oh father how your life
Has sailed the sea
Many places you have been
Now it carries me

I'm not sure of where I'm going
Except of where I've been
The sea is drifting silent
As darkness comes again

Now the cold is all around me
Like the fog, that follows rain
All my senses are exploding
As nothing stays the same

I have seen a daydream romance
Once when you were me
Chided by young innocence
That bled so hungrily

Then I never saw you
And all was left in vain
The man I never knew
As nothing stays the same

Time grew old and was soon gone
I was lifted to that land beyond
And the character of contempt
Grew to indulgence without reason
Of a fault, that was not mine

Oh father perhaps one day
You will see me
If our tides cross with the time
Perhaps you will wonder
As I did through the years

And think of me as
Your long lost son
Without shedding any tears

Starting to Fall

High on a mountain with the wind for a mane
I've been climbing so long I'm almost insane
I'm losing my balance I'm starting to fall
Will someone please help me I'm losing it all

The wind is so heavy and it's driving me back
Don't know where to turn have I lost the right track
I've been down on my luck I'm down on my knees
I'm begging for mercy oh make it end please

Don't want to go down a lost tired soul
Give me a chance so that I will know
I tried my best and gave it a fight
I don't want to lose just make it end right

High on a mountain I see the top near
Give me the strength to lose all my fear
Give me a push to try that much harder
Don't want to fall back the bottom's much farther

Starting to fall
I'm starting to fall
Will someone please help me
I'm losing it all

High on a mountain I see the top near
The wind is so heavy its bringing me tears
High on a mountain I'm starting to fall
Will someone please help me I'm losing it all

Starting to fall
I'm starting to fall
High on a mountain
I'm starting to fall

Saying Good-Bye

Saying good-bye is not easy
When you have shared a life of two
Way deep down inside
It is also hurting you

We were too demanding for each other's needs
And that I am sorry to say
What is left to do when you feel
The love is slipping away

How do we keep trying
When we can't turn a wrong into right
When we are at the end of our crossroads
Losing the will to fight

Though I hear, you call my name
Through the fog out in the distance
Your voice is growing weaker
Like a whisper fading in an instant

Saying good-bye is not easy
When you have shared a life of two
Way deep down inside
It is also hurting you

Yet we always find the courage
No matter how much the pain
To build the strength again
When we have lost just the same

So the two of us will go on broken
If only for a while
As we nurture our experience
We will gain a newfound smile

With hope one day, we will find a place
Where we can come together
To reminisce about the things we shared
Knowing they will live forever

Saying good-bye is not easy
After sharing a life of two
Way deep down inside
It is also hurting you
Hurting you

Trying to tell You

I've been trying to tell you
That it just isn't good anymore
We keep spinning in circles
Like a revolving door

Once we were hot like fire
Now we are as cold as ice
I can't take it much longer
It's making me think twice

I know that you say you love me
That you really care
How can I tell you I feel the same
When the feeling is not there

Who is there to blame if
We cannot find a way
You are making it harder
Begging me to stay

You might see it your way
I know I see it mine
I guess we did not know
How much we could be blind

Somewhere though we faltered
Losing faith in our expectations
Like voices in the darkness
Turn into shallow conversations

Though we question all the reasons
How we made it this far
I guess we were just wishing
To be each others star

So when I say so long, take care
As we part this way in time
Please don't sit and cry
You have really seen it coming
Simply say good-bye

The Beauty of You

Looking at you
A dreamer's dream
Could not be more than true
As my heart could
Be not my own

Oh, love more true
Than you could speak of
Passion in one word
Like the rising of the sun
To eternal light
Or the moon
Haloed bright
Reflecting off the silent sea
Nor to heavens' wonder
And all its mystery

And the heart
Burns with desire
Looking into
The beauty of you

Chords of Life

The chords of life surround us
We all are but it strings
Playing in a harmony
Sometimes hard to sing

Who is to say which melody
Is perfect in its score
When we seek to find a better rhythm
A little each day more

Though we seek a joyous sound
There comes at certain times
An ill struck chord of discontent
That sets it out of rhyme

Reminding us when a
Change gets added to the song
Sometimes we cannot see
If we play it, wrong

As the chords are much too many
To play an easy tune
We have to stop and listen
Or get ahead too soon

And the chords we strike are many
As we pluck and pick our strings
The highs, lows, and in betweens
The scales we learn to sing

Though each melody is different
In more than words can say
We must learn to blend
To harmonize a better way

The chords of life are many
We pluck and pick our strings
Playing in a harmony
We all must learn to sing

A Change is Near

The time has come
A change is near
No use trying to fight it
Make the move
Have to choose
Nothing to lose

Broken hearts
Familiar parts
Another day must start
Laughter, tears
Happy years
Built up walls
Echoes heard through
Empty halls

Promises made
Promises broken
A shred of memory
One last token
Once a whisper
Now a sigh
Deep breath taken
Now a cry

What you miss
A tender kiss
Nothing remains
A sad refrain
The time has come
A change is near
No use trying
To fight it

Too Little, Too Late

Too little, too late
Do we appreciate
The things we have
When taken for granted
That can't change fate

Though we try to change the
Outcome for whatever reason
We are charged a guilty plea
As trust has turned to treason

And we regret that our decision
Without a thought that has been made
To think we will be better
To stand off in the trade is

Only to be blinded by the foresight
When we see with the hindsight
Then it is too late to
Make a difference

So we carry on to save face
In the midst of growing
Contempt and confusion
While hoping for some ray of light
Will show what is real
And illusion

Tribulations

Time passes us by
As we slowly die
Moving through life's
Tribulations

And the sound of
Laughter slips through
The silence as
The darkness
Awakens

Life tempting fate
Those who don't wait
Taking it on the fast ride
Fate tempting life
Reverse of what's right
And no more tears
For those cried

Now with the
Sound of laughter
Comes a contemptuous scorn
Never really right or wrong
Somewhere in between
Then there are those
Who mourn

Funny
It all goes away
In the end

Buckroe Beach, Va.

Looking out across the ocean
The sea wind flutters
Filling me with feelings
Of nostalgia
Taking me back
To happy days
When life was easier
And the sun set warm
Against my face

When laughter and friends
Filled my life and
The summers played
Their enchantment
When the moon struck
A romantic chord
And even when it didn't

Here at Buckroe Beach
Filled within an emotion
Overflowed with time
And memories once
Thought forgotten

As the sun melts
In the distance
It's last rays reach out
To touch reminding me
Of who I am

And a sea gulls cry
Is lost in the wind

Retrospect

Been skimming through
The pages of my life
Looking back upon those days
Of youthful might
Wondering how they flew by
And why I didn't notice

Now age has fell upon me and
Wisdom has laid new plight
Sometimes wishing without regret
That I could change the outcome
To see a different light

Would it be so different
If history could refrain
Would hindsight be so vivid
Enough to make a change

Questions left unanswered
Like mysteries in the night
As the dreams of youthful splendor
Are filled with fantasies delight

Now the road we know is long
And sometimes left uncharted
As well as planned
And tried as true
Touched with disappointment

In between the ups and downs
It's not so very bad
We learn to make the best of it
And try to go unbroken

Now as these pages flutter and
Slowly come to close
My memory lingers for a moment
Filled with a little sadness
As I take the next step forward

The Silent Rapture

In the last glimmer of sunlight
Fleeting rays skip across
The silent ocean
Tenderly lapping
The rocky shore

The wind whispers
Into the dusk of night
Tickling the purple sky
Birds glide in listless motion

As stars shine
Mother Nature denudes
A feeling of oneness
As my soul is touched
With a harmony of song
And in the silent rapture
All has become one

Burning Passion Flight

The night hovered in
Convulsive agony
My mind wrought with
Shadowed perceptions and
Lingering memories of you

You
In the crystal shade of moonlight
In the creeping hollow of the dawn
In the silent cry of teardrops
In the hunger of your scorn

You
In the torment of my soul
In the tender of your touch
In the search for understanding
In the rage that bred disgust

You
In the twilights evening slumber
In the streaks of gray sunlight
In the haze of morning dewdrops
In the burning passion flight

Never once did you see
While strapped in your
Emotional confinement
Of haughty taste and
Self-repose

How your cold and
Silent measure
Crushed the delicate
World of laughter

The City Sleeps

The city sleeps tonight
Cold and hungered
In jaundiced isolation
While vagrant souls
Scour the dark and dingy
Corridors of miss-spent dreams
And forgotten tales
Of paradise lost
How sweet youth displayed

Mute whispers cry
In vain to be heard
Above the noise of
Vulgar madness
Destitute, despair
It's such an atoning
Turbulent affair

And dirges drown
The lost fleet to
Innocent pleas
Of dignity
Oh, the city sleeps tonight
But never gives up its dead

Wake up! Wake up! Wake up!
Oh decadent fever! Wake up!
The dawn will soon arise

The Silent Scream

Listen to the
Silent scream
Eerie hollow sound
Cold and desperate
Raging madness
Innocuously profound

Shudder in the
Doldrums wake
An avalanche
Tide partake of
The silence all around

Now a passion
Burning rendered
Evoking touch
That is tendered
In the silent sound

Now hear the
Silence speaking
Voices of a heart
Quickly beating

Inner thoughts
Self-depleting
Discovering the
Sense around

Hear the silence
Screaming
Lonely in the night
Its dreaming of
Wanting to be found

Blue Moon

Blue moon
Silvery night
Auspicious stars
Dancing lights

A limping wind
Pervasive scent
Wolves cry
Filled content

Interlude

Breathless
Passion
Burning bright
Summer rain
Endless night

Seasons passed
Harvest moon
A winter blue
Springtime flowers
Over you

Climbing High

Smooth movement
Climbing over the rock
Snakelike
Climbing high
Among the pinnacles
Kissing the clouds

It's a fingertip grip
With shoestring balance
Creasing the edge
On tip-toed wings
A delicate ballet
Seduction

Stretching the limits
Faced with the danger
With the challenge
With the freedom
With the rock
With myself

Nocturnal Pleasure

Hot blood running on
A Saturday night
Girls with their legs on
Check out the sights

Screaming with desire
Hot on the prowl
Full moon rising
Hear the wolves howl

Dressed in high heels
A sight for sore eyes
Its leather and lace
Its heaven in disguise

Long hair flowing
Catching the breeze
The seduction is rising
Like an incurable disease

Red lips pouting
Hungry for a taste
Savor the moment
Nothing goes to waste

Now the temperature is rising
Are you ready for more
Come on baby
Open the store

Its perfumed passion
Drawing the scent
Its nocturnal pleasure
And the night
Drenched in sweat

Childhood Lost

I remember the days when I was free
The years of a simple life, that carried me
They all seem to run so fast
Childhood innocence of the past

In the land that time forgot are
Those special places of forget me not's
Deep within my heart still reigns
Those make believe childhood games

Now there is a place where I once stood still
When I climbed upon that magic hill
And there in my dreams of an innocent, age
I conquered the world on that primordial stage

I opened the doors to sights unseen
I slew the dragon for my beauty queen
I climbed mountain peaks and flew the sky
I traveled beyond the highest high

Yet as fate would have it, the dreams would end
I would not go back again
For a boy to a man must come to pass
And leave behind the innocence at last

Deep inside my heart still reigns
Those make believe childhood games
When I climb upon that magic hill
There is a place where I stand still

For the man becomes a boy once more
To live again like before
For in the wake of childhood lost
The boy becomes a man at a worldly cost

First Embrace

Under the moon
A first embrace
A starry night
Of midnight lace

A tender touch
Impassioned kiss
Secret whispers
From your lips

Turquoise eyes
Set afire
Speak of longing
And desire

Tempted passion
Feelings burn
The moon cries out
Bodies yearn

This Passage

When you feel your world is crumbling
And no one seems to care
Who is it you can turn to
When no one is there

Must you travel down life's quilted road
In dusky isolation
Why can't you find some peace of mind
One bit of compensation

You have been hurt and broken
You have been left for dead
You have sought the loving warm embrace
Only to find the coldness of the heart instead

You have been torn and shattered
You have risen from the ash
You have licked and tendered wounds
Without offers of help asked

You have found the strength
To carry on
Overcome the weakness and
Found the will was strong

Or maybe it is pride that's talking
That says you must survive
Even if it means your life seems
Only half alive

Now I ask that this passage
Will surely come to end
For in this life I have to give
Is much more than I can lend

Don't Look Now

I feel you in the rushing wind
Got my head all in a spin
Don't look now but I think I am
I am falling in love again

Don't think twice about the way I feel
The moon and the stars have no doubt
The nights allure is coming out
Don't look now I think I am
I am falling in love again

You must think I am crazy
That my mind must be a little hazy
That maybe I am a fool but Baby
I am a fool for you

Don't turn away its not too soon
I don't want a heartache in winter
When it's the middle of June
Stay awhile and see where we go
Come on Baby we'll win, place, and show
Don't look now

I can see the wonder in your eyes
How it took me by surprise
Let there be no thought uncertain
You are the one who pulled back the curtain
Surrounding my lonely heart

In the mirror of sunshine
I see your reflection
Like a beacon in the night
My heart is coming in your direction
Don't look now Baby, don't look now

I feel you in the rushing wind
Got my head all in a spin
Don't look now I think I am
I am falling in love again

Don't look now Baby
Don't look now
I'm a fool for you
Baby don't look now

One Dream

I saw you picking through the rubble
Of life's lost and broken dreams
Searching for one of your own
Funny how many fall through the seams
How many turn to stone

    Well dreams may come and dreams may go
    When we were young how could we know
    Some dreams would live and some would die
    Some dreams we would never get to try

You know as we get older
Some dreams fade away with time
Not really catching sight
Not really yours or mine

    Does it really matter how many dreams fall through
    As long as there is one dream
    That still belongs to you
    You have to believe with all your heart
    That you can make it true

Because it's:
    One dream to hold a future bright
    One dream in the first breath of life
    One dream in the hearts of the young
    One dream in the rising sun

It's one dream at the rainbows end
One dream in the hands of a friend
One dream in the fading light
One dream in the lonely night

> It's one dream to plant a growing seed
> One dream for the hungry to feed
> One dream for the sick and the poor
> One dream to find a common cure

It's one dream where the down-trodden lay
One dream for the birth of a new day
One dream that turns a wrong to right
One dream that brings new sight

> It's one dream for the righteous cause
> One dream no more hatred and wars
> One dream for the brotherhood of man
> One dream for peace throughout the land

It's one dream for the love of us all
One dream for the world to call
One dream to reach the mountain top
One dream to never stop

> One dream one heart beating with life
> Don't tear it apart
> One dream for you and for me
> One dream for everyone to see
> For everyone to be free

If You Have To Leave

There is this feeling in the air
Or do I sense it in your stare
That the love light
In your eyes is fading

I ask you if it's true as
You turn your head away
You say that you can't stay
That the love is gone
That it's over

Oh, won't you love me, like,
The way you did before
Hold me close once more
Tell me I'm not dreaming

I don't want to see you go
Honey, don't you know
How much I love you
My heart is screaming

Well if you have to leave
I just can't conceive
What to do without you
You are all the world to me

Now the feeling is not the same
The love has turned to pain
Oh, won't you hold me in your arms
If for one more time
I'll pretend that you're still mine

Now the night is still as
The tears begin to break my will
I'm falling to my knees
Oh Darling won't you please
Think it over

Well if you have to leave
I just can't conceive
What to do without you
If you have to leave
I just can't conceive
How to live without you

Once and Then

I loved you once and then
In the summer of my youth
In the cool waters of
My dreams you flowed
You languished in the
Marrow of my soul
My first love

You poured into my veins
Like blood upon the earth
Although you did not know it
You crept into my heart like
Dawn steals the nights embrace
Although you did not know it

And now
The softness of your touch
The linger of your kiss
The beauty of your smile
Come back to me
In the night of my years
Since passed

You
In the shadow of my memory
In the trace of dawn
In the stillness, that surrounds me
In the echoes of my heart

I loved you once and then
In the summer of my youth
I love you now

Look at the Night

Look! Look!
Look at the night
The mysterious night
Ahhh! The seduction of
Your voluminous depth
Take me to your breast

Virgin night
You succor the fantasies
Of the daylight and
The wind moans
With desire
Sighing of the pleasure
Wrap yourself around me
Engulf me with
Your treasure

Wanton night
Oh woman you are
I beckon to your call
Without ever really
Having you

Oh but for the madness
The madness that drives us
The madness of us all

Look at the night
The mysterious night
Beckon to her call

Different Drummer

Fate is dealt in the cards we play
Destiny lies in the wind
Everything has its reason
No matter how we come
Where we go or
What is left behind

Life charts its unknown course
As we pick and choose
To follow each beat of
That different drummer

Let it not be left unsaid
As we continue to grow older
Sometimes in the maze we face
We wish that we could be
Just a little younger

Then, how we would march to
The tune of a different drummer

Your Eyes

It was the intensity
Of your eyes that moved me
Those, fire breathing dragon eyes
Mahogany rich, mystery eyes

Sensuous, penetrating
Melt me all over eyes
Your gaze to tantalize
But for one sweet caress

I get lost in your eyes
Those, mesmerizing eyes
Pouring deep into
My soul eyes

I drown, in your eyes
Those, dressed to kill
Kind of eyes
Reflecting the night
Moon bright eyes

It was your eyes
The intensity
Of your eyes
That moved me

Take Me Away

Take me away
To someplace not so near
Take me where
There is not a care

Far, far beyond that border
Where freedom reigns
And there are no chains
Of life's complexity

Take me far from that
Contaminating seed
No polluted stains
Against a bright horizon

Take me where the dreams
Oh, the dreams are alive
And life is like
A new day rising

Oh, take me to that
Golden place of
Tranquil and serene
Where the rivers meet
The seas embrace
And caress the
Shores abiding

Oh, take me where
The heart is true
And love is not forlorn
Take me to that land
Way, way, way over yonder

Where freedom reigns
And there are no chains
And life is full
Of naked wonder

But For a Kiss

But for a kiss upon
Your tender lips
That I do ask to taste
The vintage wine

A kiss, a kiss upon
Your virgin lips
Pressed to the
Heart of mine

Oh, succulent surrender
Ripe as brandied fruit
Not to kiss a
Thousand times
But once, just once to
Drink the sweetened nectar

Oh, but for a kiss
One tender kiss
That I do ask to
Lay your lips on mine

Dear lady,
Just one kiss to
Last throughout
All time

Lonely State of Mind

Why do I think about you
Is it my lonely state of mind
After all, we are two strangers
You consume me all the time

    Why do I think about you
    Imagining your touch
    After all, you hardly know me
    This rage is like an infectious crush

What exactly is it
That attracts me so
Although I hardly know you
Still I would like to know

    Is it in your smile
    The perfume that you wear
    The way you look at me
    Is it the way you walk
    The sound of your voice
    Is it just my fantasy

Is it the way your lips
Tremble with emotion
The way your eyes shine
In the light
Is it just a dream I see
In the lonely night

Is it the thought
Of making love to feel
Your body close to mine
To whisper secret nothings
To feel the love again
Or am I wasting time

Although I hardly know you
You consume me still
Like an endless river
About to break my will

Is it in your smile
The perfume that you wear
The way you look at me
Is it just my fantasy or

My lonely state of mind
My lonely state of mind
My lonely state of mind
Lonely state of mind

In the Land of Dreams

I was human once
In the land of dreams
And make-believe
Riding giant see-saws
In a wave of
Diametrical destiny
Burdened by the outcome
Of lost innocence being
Played out in real time

Naked woman stalked the streets
As I fell victim to the matter
Surrounded by those so called
Helping hands of opportunity
Being the devil in disguise

You know some of you mentors are
Not really very good at it so
I took it upon myself to
Discover what the real meaning
Might have been
Taking what I could
Leaving the rest behind

Now shoot me through that cannon
Drop me at the door
Give me that one quick fix
So I won't go back there anymore

Well you know that
I am still human and
I have so much
More to learn

In the land of dreams
And make-believe
Riding giant see-saws

A Love Gone By

Bittersweet memories
Days gone by of you and me
Fading into history
A love gone by and you wonder why
A love gone by like a river runs dry

We held so much promise
When we were young
We thought we were the fortunate ones
Did we lose everything in the sun

Where did we go my Darling
Where did we go my Dear
Thinking of you my Darling
Seems like a better place than here

A love gone by and you wonder why
A love gone by like a river runs dry
We held so much promise
When we were young
We thought we were the fortunate ones
Did we lose everything in the sun

Where are you now my Darling
Where are you now my Dear
Voices of the past keep haunting me
Today keeps on taunting me and
I am wishing you were here
Wishing you were near

If only for a moment
To feel your condolence
To see your smiling face again
To feel your touch again
To hear your words again
To help make my world again
A better place in time

Those bittersweet memories
Are fading into history
Days gone by of you and me
A love gone by of you and me
A love gone by

Crossroads

And so I am standing here
In that early evening light
Staring at the crossroads
Of my mid-term life

I have come so far yet still have
A long, long way to go
Though at times it's been a burden
Still I would like to know

What lies ahead for me
Which way do I turn
I have to take that step I know
There is so much more to learn

Now there lies this hesitation
I'm on the edge of dark uncertainty
Or maybe it's procrastination
As I wonder, what, is in store for me

Oh, what lies ahead in waiting
Of all those things unseen
Will I fall into the darkness
Will I stumble by the way
Will I crawl upon my hands and knees
To find a brighter day

Will I rise above to greatness
Will I reach the mountain top
Will I come to find new meaning
Of what life holds for me
What is my destiny

So I stand here at the crossroads
In that early evening light
Hesitating, looking back upon my life
I have come so far yet still have
A long, long way to go
A long, long way to go

A Bright Tomorrow

When the time has come for me to go
And death calls out my name
I only hope that I can say
My life was not lived out in vain

I hope I did the right thing
When faced with adversity
That I stepped up to the challenge
And when wrong not be judged to harshly

I hope that there was purpose
In everything I've done
Despite my faults and my mistakes
I blame myself bar none

If there were, ever any feelings hurt
In the paths I crossed along the way
Please know it was without malice or intent
And I hope you find your peace someday

I hope that I leave something
Something good behind
That when I am remembered
It might be just and kind

I hope that you will know
That I tried my very best
Upon the peaks and in the valleys
Throughout my life's contest

So when the time has come for me to go
And death calls out my name
Please do not mourn for me in sorrow
Celebrate a life well lived
And know, I always hoped
For a bright tomorrow

Forever and a Day

I know I can't make you love me
I know I can't make you stay
But if it could be for just one minute
Could it be forever and a day

Darling you know that I love you
You know I will always be true
Like the stars and the moon above you
There is nothing I wouldn't do

Oh if I could make the magic
And spill loves fragrance in the air
If I could make the love shine
Would you see it in my stare

Would you feel the beating of my heart
Pounding faster each and every minute
Or like the ocean crashing on the shore
And see the beauty that is in it

Would you hear my voice tremble in a whisper
Or like the roaring of the wind
Or like the love birds calling
When the spring time comes again

Would you feel my caress upon you
In the tingling of my touch
Like a thousand moonlight kisses
And know, I love you, oh, so much

If I could make you love me
If I could make you stay
I would make it for just one minute
Forever and a day

If I Could Change the World

If I could change the world
To make it just a better place
Full of love and no more prejudice or hate
Instead of fighting all the bloody wars
We would be fighting for a better cause

No more poverty or disease
No more prison walls or boundaries
No more anger, no more fear
No more children crying tears

No more lies, deceit, or pain
No more guilt, no more shame
No more wrong and no more hunger
We would help the weak become stronger

No more darkness, no despair
No more blame, no lack of care
No more racism, no more greed
No more sorrow, no more need
No more injustice or inequality
We would fight for the truth
From sea to sea

If I could change the world
To make it just a better place
Full of love and no more prejudice or hate
Would you come with me to make that stand
As we travel toward the Promised Land
We'll plant a seed for the future bright
For all to see in the guiding light

If I, could change the world

Grand Canyon

I stood upon the precipice
And gazed across
The vast immense
In beauty of
Such words denied
My soul in yearning
Cried and cried

And begged my heart
For what to say
In which my eyes
Could not convey
Surrounded in
The wonderment
Undeniably heaven sent

Oh, what truth lies before me
Others may not see
Of what divine impression
Stamped across eternity

Might I find the words to fill
This vast immense before me
Like thunder rolls across the golden plain
To the deepest reaches
Of its smallest grain
Mired inside the beauty
Caught in awestruck wonder

And in the silence
Of where I stand
I have touched
Gods' palatal hand

Crazy

Crazy, that's what I am for you
Crazy and I don't know what to do
You went away and took my heart
I'm drowning in the deepest blue

Crazy, all those things you said
Keep running through my head
Funny, you never meant a word
Or was it something
Something else I heard

Crazy, I would do anything for you
To make your dreams come true
I would climb a mountain high
Swim the oceans' tide
Just for you

In the darkest night
I would shine the brightest light
And in the raging storm
Be your fortress strong
Just for you
Just for you

Crazy, you were the flame
That sparked a fire
Deep within my hearts desire
There inside your sweet caress
The touch of longing tenderness
Then you left

Crazy, that's what I am for you
Crazy and I don't know what to do
You went away and took my heart
But I'll get over you
I'll, get over you
Crazy

If I Could Find the Words to Tell You

If I could find the words to tell you
To bring you peace of mind to quell you
Of all your doubt and fear
To bring your heart from crying tears

If I could paint a world of beauty
Just for you to see
Full of joy and love and happiness
To truly set you free

If I could build a rock for you to stand on
To give you courage and strength
If I could show you all the universe
On an ounce of faith

If I could make your dreams come true
To fulfill all that you desire
If I could grant one wish
Just to take you higher

I would say it in a word like Socrates or Plato
I would paint heaven's paradise above
I would build a castle from a single grain of sand
I would wish you faith to take you higher

And your dreams would come true like magic
All falling into place unfettered
There we would stand eye to eye
And soul to soul embraced

Some People

Some people see in colors, some in black and white
Some refuse to see the truth between the wrong and right
Some people are made of plastic some are made of stone
Some preach about the righteousness from their holy throne

Some people tell you stories some tell you lies
Some people wear false faces to hide in the disguise
Some use you for whatever they can get
Some play with your emotions and just as soon forget

Some people make excuses some pass the blame
Some think nothing of living inside the shame
Some people cry for help, some never listen
Some wait to get their fix on what you are missing

Some live, like there is no tomorrow, some live inside a shell
Some only confuse you it is all so hard to tell
Some criticize and judge you and laugh at you instead
Some people are walking wounded some are living dead

Some people take more than what they give
Some struggle through each day to find a way to live
Some people shine their light afar
Some only wish upon a star

Some people get swallowed up in anger
Some get swallowed up in pain
Like a monkey on your back
That is driving you insane

Some people are blinded by their envy
Some by their prejudice and hate
Some wrap you in a box blinded by perception
As they sign and seal your fate

Some people, well, you know who they are
They are sitting all around us
They are in your local bar
They are driving down the highway
They are walking in the street
The rich man, poor man, the beggar man, and thief
The next lover or friend that you meet

Now some people will pay these words no mind
Trapped within some prison as they do their time
Some will twist these words around unwilling
To admit it as they search for a higher ground

Some people will stand above the rest but
Those lines that separate us can be a twisted, tangled mess
Are we so much different from others that we see
You know there are some people just like you and me

Some people see in colors, some in black and white

Moody Girl

She's such a moody girl
Running through the
Shadows of the night
She's closed her world
But her eyes still hold a trace
Of that burning light

She's given up on love
She pretends to smile, puts on a front
Trying to be tough
She can't hide the weakness inside
Her empty heart cries
Lost on the wings of love

A broken trust lies in the dust
Torn by the thorns of a love betrayed
And she wonders will it ever come again
Will she find the strength to begin again

She's down, down on love
And I wonder has she really given up
Will she ever open up
Moody girl, oh moody girl,
Like a mystery in the night
Will you ever shine, shine your light

She's such a moody girl
She doesn't really see
How she makes my world
She's a moody girl
Living in a lonely world

Moody girl, oh moody girl
Please don't you cry
I'll be strong for you
Moody girl, oh moody girl
Won't you breathe a sigh
I'll be there for you

Moody girl, oh moody girl
She's such a moody girl
Running through the
Shadows of the night

If Dreams Had Wings

December snow is falling
Moonlight is breaking through
Whispers of the wind comes calling
Bringing dreams of you
And if dreams had wings I'd be flying
Flying to you

You might think that I am crazy
It has been so long I know
Still, there is something deep inside
That doesn't let you go

Maybe it is the loneliness
As I've wandered through the years
Searching for that love I never seem to find
Up and down and all around
For a little peace of mind
And if dreams had wings I'd be flying
Flying to you

We were young and innocent what did we really know
We were wild and free and our hearts in love did grow
There were dreams to fill in that early till
As our hearts became entwined
We looked upon the star of hope
There the future shined
And if dreams had wings I'd be flying
Flying to you

You moved to California
Your daddy called it home
And the dreams tumbled down like stone
You sent me one last letter
Said that you still loved me that it was too far
Said you gave up on the dreams
But still wished upon that star
Said you found someone new
Three thousand miles away
And I couldn't get to you, get to you

I'm still this restless wanderer
I thought I would let you know
There is something deep inside
That doesn't let you go
And if dreams had wings I'd be flying
Flying to you

Stand By You

When the night is long and the day begins to dawn
When you find yourself so all alone
Between a heartache and a love
That you can call your own

When the light appears and the end is not in sight
And your world begins to crumble
When a broken heart causes you to stumble
When the tears begin to fall
When you think that, you have lost it all

Don't be so sad wash away your blue
I'll be the one to stand by you
Stand by you

I'll pick you up when you are down
I'll give you strength to carry on
I'll build your confidence until you are strong
I'll bring you smiles as far as you can see
You can count on me

When the storm is raging
And you have that inner doubt
When that sea of confusion
Won't let you think it out
When you find yourself so all alone
When there is no place, you call home

When you feel like you can't hang on
When you have lost all of your will and desire
When you feel like it's the end of the fire
When the tears begin to fall
When you think that, you have lost it all

Don't be so sad wash away your blue
I'll be the one to stand by you
Stand by you

I'll be there by your side
You will never have to hide
I'll never let you fall you'll see
I'll give you all I have of me

Don't be so sad wash away your blue
I'll be the one to stand by you
Stand by you.
I'll be the one to stand by you

Find My Way

Sunday morning, three a.m.
Where do I begin
These lonely nights without you
Sure are wearing thin

Since you've been gone
I haven't been the same
I've been lost and aimless
Drowning in this rain

I've been waiting for the sun to shine
For the light of day
Don't you know without you
I can't seem to find my way

I've been living on those dreams
We used to talk about
Lying broken in the shadows
While my heart just screams and shouts

The ghost of you still haunts me
As I'm imagining your touch
Baby don't you know
I'm still loving you so much
Still loving you so much

Everything keeps passing by
Spinning all so fast
Caught inside this downward spiral
Oh Lord, please don't make it last

I've been waiting for the sun to shine
For the light of day
Don't you know without you
I can't seem to find my way

Find my way
Find my way
I can't seem to find my way

Motorcycle Mama

She made her entrance
Slow and deliberate
Straddled on bucking
Heavy metal madness

Hot steel stallion
Rumbling, rabid
Sweet deliverance
Sensuously,
She penetrated
The crowd

Her raven hair swept back
Tasted the wind
Her eyes hidden in
Shades of midnight
Her lips pursed
Ready to strike

Hypnotized
The temperature rose
In a caldron of desire
Wanting to know,
Her name

Winners and Losers

Cars, trucks, and
Motorcycles
Weave in and out
Race down life's
Two-lane highway
High-speed chase

Hustlers running the beat
Pimping the street
Jockey for position
Through that
Ancient gauntlet

Cheers muted by the
Roar of engines
Tires screech to
Destinations
On a fast track
Sometimes going
Nowhere

Stoplights
Wave us on and
White lines mired in
Swollen parking lots
Become asphalt
Winner circles

Winners and losers all
Someone, somewhere
Cheers us on

New Birth

I went inside
My mind scattered
A river of roses
Lay tattered
Spilling red scent
Through emerald
Forests

In pools of fire
Comes the dawn
Do you know when
Her death was born

Into the marrow
Of mother earth
Cries
And we arise
From the shallows

Clinging to the
Bosom of creation